Eruption!

THE STORY OF VOLCANOES

Written by Anita Ganeri

Penguin
Random
House

Series Editor Deborah Lock
Editor Pomona Zaheer
Art Editors C. David Gillingwater, Dheeraj Arora
Senior Art Editor Clare Shedden
US Editors Regina Kahney, Shannon Beatty
Production Editor Siu Chan
Producer, Pre-production Francesca Wardell
Picture Researchers Marie Osborn, Sumedha Chopra
Jacket Designer Natalie Godwin
DTP Designer Anita Yadav
Managing Editor Soma B. Chowdhury
Managing Art Editor Ahlawat Gunjan
Indexer Lynn Bresler

Reading Consultant
Linda Gambrell, Ph.D.

First American Edition, 2001
Other editions, 2010
This edition, 2015
Published in the United States by DK Publishing
345 Hudson Street, New York, New York 10014

15 16 17 18 19 10 9 8 7 6 5 4 3 2 1
001—270538—June/15

A catalog record for this book is available
from the Library of Congress.

ISBN: 978-1-4654-3579-8 (Paperback)
ISBN: 978-1-4654-3578-1 (Hardcover)

DK books are available at special discounts when purchased in bulk for sales promotions,
premiums, fund-raising, or educational use. For details, contact:
DK Publishing Special Markets
345 Hudson Street, New York, New York 10014
SpecialSales@dk.com

Printed and bound in China

The publisher would like to thank the following for their kind permission to reproduce their photographs:
(Key: a=above, b=below/bottom, c=center, l=left, r=right, t=top)

Alamy Images: Janusz Gniadek 29, Christian Kober / Robert Harding World Imagery 28cl, Meir Levavi / PhotoStock-Israel
29cl, Photo Resource Hawaii / Bluegreen Pictures 4–5b, 28, Martin Rietze / Stocktrek Images 27tr, Greg Vaughn 27cl;
Dorling Kindersley: Bethany Dawn / Bethany Dawn 26cla; **Dreamstime.com:** Selitbul 29bl; **Getty Images:** Arya Bima /
AFP 28bl, Leemage 40br, Panoramic Images 27tl, Sadatsugu Tomizawa / AFP 28clb, Greg Vaughn / Perspectives 5crb;
Corbis UK Ltd: Front jacket, 24br, 38tc, 39. **Ecoscene:** 30cb. **Robert Harding Picture Library:** 1, 19, 20–21, Rolly Pedrina
29clb. **N.H.P.A.:** Brian Hawks 35. **Oxford Scientific Films:** Anne Head 18. **Pa Photos:** 6. **Planet Earth Pictures:** 17, 23c,
31tc; Dorian Wiesel 37. **Science Photo Library:** 7; David Halpern 33; NASA 27crb, Peter Ryan 34. **Frank Spooner
Pictures:** 11. **Tony Stone Images:** Back jacket, 9. **Topham Picturepoint:** 16tc, 22bc.
Jacket images: *Front:* **National Geographic Stock:** Carsten Peter
Back: **Dorling Kindersley:** Natural History Museum, London tr.
All other images © Dorling Kindersley
For further information see: www.dkimages.com

A WORLD OF IDEAS
SEE ALL THERE IS TO KNOW

www.dk.com

Contents

Be a Volcano Ranger

First-hand real adventures!

- ✓ Learn about volcanoes.
- ✓ Help to take care of volcano national parks.
- ✓ Share your learning with others.

Win a certificate!

Things you can do:

- watch an eruption from a safe distance.

- collect interesting volcanic rocks.

- hike to the rim of a volcano.

- walk through lava tubes.

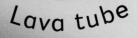

Lava tube

What looks like a mountain
but spits out fire?
What shoots clouds of smoke
from a hole in its top?
What sometimes explodes
with a BANG?

A volcano
and it's starting to erupt!

7

The story of a volcano
starts underground.
If you jump up and down
on the ground,
it feels solid and hard.

But inside the earth,
it is so hot that the rocks melt.
The rocks are runny
like melted butter.

Sometimes the melted rock
bursts up through a hole
or a crack in the ground.
This is how a volcano begins.

The rock that comes out of
a volcano is called lava.
At first, it is runny
and red-hot.
It cools down
in the air
and turns into
hard, black rock.

Cooled lava

Some volcanoes spurt out
fiery fountains of lava.
Other volcanoes pour out lava
in great rivers of fire.
Once the lava starts flowing,
nothing can stop it.
It can bury whole villages
and set trees and
houses on fire.

Make a Volcano Model

To make an erupting cone-shaped volcano, you will need: a bottle, a tray, sand, baking soda, red food coloring, dishwashing liquid, and vinegar. You can decorate your volcano with plants, stones, and toy animals.

1 Place the bottle on the tray.

2 Build a mound of sand around the bottle. Keep the hole open.

3 Now place plants, stones, and toy animals around the volcano.

4 Mix together the baking soda, red food coloring, and dishwashing liquid in the bottle. Then pour in vinegar. Watch your volcano erupt!

Volcanoes have different shapes
and sizes.

Some volcanoes erupt with a bang.

Hot rocks and ash
shoot high into the air.

These volcanoes form
cone-shaped mountains
with steep sides.

Other volcanoes erupt quietly.
The lava oozes gently out of the top
and spreads out all around.
These volcanoes are low and wide.

Some volcanoes erupt violently.
They blast out
clouds of hot ash and dust.
The ash is made of
tiny pieces of lava.
The ash and dust
shoot high into the air.
Some of it lands near the volcano.
It covers buildings and fields
in thick, dark gray powder.

Some ash and dust is carried away
by the wind.
It can block out the sun
and turn day into night.

At the top of a volcano
is a hollow called a crater.
In it is a hole called the vent.
Lava, ash, and dust
come out of the vent.
Some craters are many miles
(kilometers) wide.

When a volcano stops erupting,
the crater is left.
Some old craters fill up with water
to form huge lakes.
Sometimes the crater becomes
a dry, grassy plain.

When a volcano shoots out lava and ash, we say that it is erupting. We call a volcano that is erupting "active."

Kilauea (KILL–uh–WAY–uh)
in Hawaii is the most active
volcano on earth.
It has erupted
non–stop
since 1983!

We call a volcano that is not
erupting "dormant."
That means it is sleeping,
but it could erupt at any time.
Montserrat is a tiny island
in the Caribbean Sea.
It used to be a beautiful place
to live.
Then, in 1995, a volcano called
Chance's Peak started to erupt.

It had been dormant for 400 years.
Many people had to leave
their homes as ash fell everywhere.
Some left the island
and went to live
in another country.
It was too dangerous
for them to stay.

Volcanic ash

Mount Vesuvius (Veh–SOO–vee–uss)
is a volcano in Italy.
In AD 79, Mount Vesuvius
erupted violently, blasting hot ash
and gas into the air.
The ash buried the town
of Pompeii (Pom–PAY) and
thousands of people died.
Today, people have cleared
the ash away.
You can walk around
the streets of Pompeii and
see the Roman ruins.

*A cast of a dog
covered by the ash.*

The ruins of the
Roman town of Pompeii

Record Holders

Many volcanoes are famous for their eruptions and size. Here are some of the record holders.

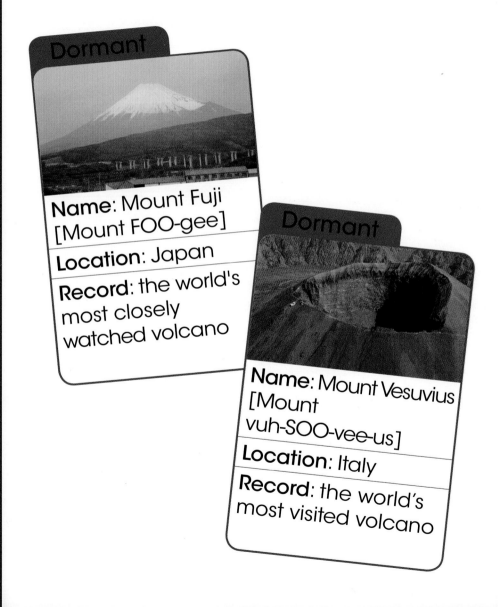

Dormant

Name: Mount Fuji [Mount FOO-gee]

Location: Japan

Record: the world's most closely watched volcano

Dormant

Name: Mount Vesuvius [Mount vuh-SOO-vee-us]

Location: Italy

Record: the world's most visited volcano

Name: Mauna Loa
[MAW-nuh LOW-uh]

Location: Hawaii, USA

Record: the biggest volcano on Earth

Name: Krakatoa
[CRACK-uh-TOE-uh]

Location: Indonesia

Record: produced the loudest bang ever heard when it erupted in 1883

Name: Kilauea
[KILL-uh-WAY-uh]

Location: Hawaii, USA

Record: the most active volcano on Earth

Name: Olympus Mons
[uh-LIM-puhs mons]

Location: Mars

Record: the biggest volcano in the known universe

Volcanoes: The Bad and the Good

Volcanoes can be very dangerous and set off other disasters. However, they can also be useful.

Earthquake
A volcano can sometimes set off an earthquake. Violent earthquakes can destroy cities and kill people.

Tsunami
A volcanic eruption can cause a giant water wave called a tsunami. The wave destroys everything in its way.

Weather disruption
When a volcano erupts, gas and dust are thrown up. This can blot out the sunlight, and cause strong winds and heavy rainfall.

Pumice stone

Rocks
Some volcanic rocks are useful. Pumice is used to rub away hard skin. Basalt is used to make building blocks and sidewalks.

Farming
Eruptions clear away old, dead plants. Volcanic ash makes the soil rich for strong and healthy plant growth.

Hot springs
In some volcanic regions, people use hot underground water to heat their homes and make electricity.

Volcanoes can be useful.
On the slopes of volcanoes,
the soil is good for growing crops.

In some places, blocks of solid lava
are used to build roads,
bridges, and houses.
Precious gold
and diamonds
are found in some
volcanic rock.

Near a volcano,
the underground rocks get very hot.
The hot rocks heat up water,
which turns to steam.
Sometimes a giant jet
of boiling water and steam
bursts up through the ground
and into the air.
The jet is called a geyser.

Old Faithful is a famous geyser
in Yellowstone Park, Wyoming.
It got its name because it always
bursts up once every hour.

There are lots of volcanoes
under the sea.
You can't see most of them.
But some underwater volcanoes
are so tall that they poke up
from the sea to make islands.

In 1963, a volcano erupted
under the sea near Iceland.
The sea started to smoke and steam.
By the next day,
the volcano had grown
and a brand-new island had formed.
The local people called it Surtsey,
named after an
Icelandic fire god.

Hawaii is a group of more than
100 islands in the Pacific Ocean.
The islands are the tops
of huge underwater volcanoes.
Some of these volcanoes have
two or more craters,
but they erupt very gently.

In some places,
lava flows into the sea
and makes it hiss and steam.
Some of the beaches have
black sand, which is made from
crushed-up lava.

Volcanologists (VUL-can-AHL-uh-gists) are scientists who try to find out how volcanoes work.
They want to know when volcanoes are going to erupt.
Then people living nearby can be moved to safety.

But volcanologists have not found all the answers yet.

No one knows when a volcano will erupt—until it actually does!

Volcanic Myths

In myths, volcanic eruptions are caused by gods and goddesses.

Vulcan [VOL-ken]
In Roman myths, he is the god of fire and crafts. The word "volcano" comes from his name. Vulcan's Greek name is **Hephaestus** [hef-EEST-us].
In myths, he is lame, so he hides away in his workshops, which are under volcanoes. There, he heats and shapes metals.

Pele [PEY-ley]
She is the Hawaiian goddess of volcanoes. The legends say that a volcano erupts when Pele gets angry.

Surtur [SERT-er]
He is the Icelandic god of fire. The volcanic island of Surtsey is named after him.

Fuchi [FOO-chee]
She is the Japanese goddess of fire. Mount Fuji is named after her.

Rise to the Top

See if you can find your way out of this volcano. Answer the questions correctly and you will!

Hot

Cool

What is the melted rock that comes out of a volcano called?

In the air

Start

Where does an eruption start?

Underground

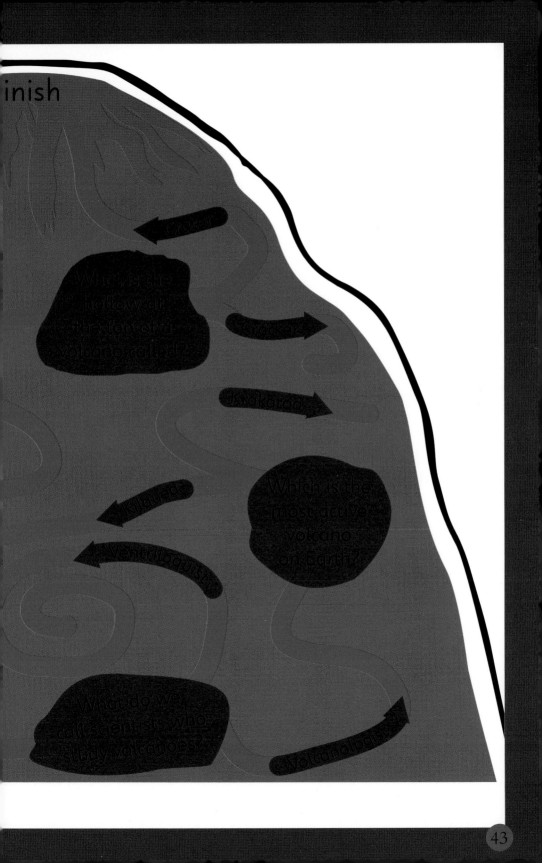

Crater

What is the hollow at the top of a volcano called?

Cracka →

Krakatoa →

← Kilauea

← Ventriloquist

Which is the most active volcano on Earth?

What do we call scientists who study volcanoes?

Volcanologists →

Glossary

active
volcano that often
erupts

ash
tiny pieces of volcanic
rock

crater
dip at the opening
of a volcano from
where gas, lava,
and ash come out

dormant
volcano that has not
erupted in a long time
but will erupt again

eruption
when lava and ash
shoot out of a volcano

extinct
volcano that has
stopped erupting and
will not erupt again

geyser
sudden jet of boiling
water and steam

lava
hot, melted rock that
comes out of a volcano

tsunamis
giant water waves
that can be caused
by volcanic eruptions
or earthquakes

volcanologist
scientist who studies
volcanoes

Index

45

Guide for Parents

DK Readers is a four-level interactive reading adventure series for children, developing the habit of reading widely for both pleasure and information. These books have an exciting main narrative interspersed with a range of reading genres to suit your child's reading ability, as required by the Common Core State Standards. Each book is designed to develop your child's reading skills, fluency, grammar awareness, and comprehension in order to build confidence and engagement when reading.

Ready for a *Beginning to Read Alone* book

YOUR CHILD SHOULD

- be able to read many words without needing to stop and break them down into sound parts.
- read smoothly, in phrases and with expression.
  By this level, your child will be beginning to read silently.
- self-correct when a word or sentence doesn't sound right.

A VALUABLE AND SHARED READING EXPERIENCE

For some children, text reading, particularly non-fiction, requires much effort, but adult participation can make this both fun and easier. So here are a few tips on how to use this book with your child.

TIP 1 Check out the contents together before your child begins:

- invite your child to check the blurb, contents page, and layout of the book and comment on it.
- ask your child to make predictions about the story.
- talk about the information your child might want to find out.

TIP 2 Encourage fluent and flexible reading:

- support your child to read in fluent, expressive phrases, making full use of punctuation and thinking about the meaning.

- help your child learn to read with expression by choosing a sentence to read aloud and demonstrating how to do this.

TIP 3 **Indicators that your child is reading for meaning:**
- your child will be responding to the text if he/she is self-correcting and varying his/her voice.
- your child will want to talk about what he/she is reading or is eager to turn the page to find out what will happen next.

TIP 4 **Chat at the end of each chapter:**
- encourage your child to recall specific details after each chapter.
- let your child pick out interesting words and discuss what they mean.
- talk about what each of you found most interesting or most important.
- ask questions about the text. These help to develop comprehension skills and awareness of the language used.

A FEW ADDITIONAL TIPS
- Read to your child regularly to demonstrate fluency, phrasing, and expression; to find out or check information; and for sharing enjoyment.
- Encourage your child to reread favorite texts to increase reading confidence and fluency.
- Check that your child is reading a range of different types of material, such as poems, jokes, and following instructions.

Series consultant, **Dr. Linda Gambrell**, Distinguished Professor of Education at Clemson University, has served as President of the National Reading Conference, the College Reading Association, and the International Reading Association. She is also reading consultant for the **DK Adventures**.

Have you read these other great books from DK?

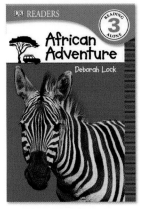

Embark on a mission to explore the solar system. First stop—Mars.

Join Louise at the zoo, helping to welcome a new panda baby.

Eat or be eaten! Step back in time to when dinosaurs roamed Earth.

Meet the sharks who live on the reef or come passing through.

Experience the thrill of seeing wild animals on an African safari.

Through Zoe's blog, discover the mysteries of the Amazon.